SOURCE

THE GENESIS OF SUCCESS IN BUSINESS AND LIFE

DR. MARC B. COOPER

Calligraphy by Jue Pu

Seeking Wisdom LLC

Portland, Oregon

SOURCE: The Genesis of
Success in Business and Life
Text Copyright © 2018
by Dr. Marc B. Cooper

All Rights Reserved.

Published by Sahalie Press

Woodenville, Washington

No part of this publication may be reproduced in whole or in part, or stored in a retrieval system, or transmitted in nany form or by any means, electronic, mechanical, photocopyinng, recordingn or otherwise, without permission in nwritingn from Seeking-Wisdom LLC, except by a reviewer who may quote brief passages.

For longer quotations, permission requests may be addressed to info@seeking-wisdom.com.

Seeking Wisdom LLC, USA

Library of Congress Control Number: 2008938635

ISBN: 9781979715522

Printed in the USA

Third Edition, 2018

Editing by Matthew King

*A short saying
often contains much wisdom.*

SOPHO
CLES

INTRODUCTION

What I have discovered in almost three decades of consulting, coaching and training successful professionals is that possessing a clear understanding of who you are is far more decisive than a business plan. You do, in fact, need to make plans, set goals, define objectives, and develop smart strategies, but that is not what ultimately drives achievement and success. What provides that germination for success exists at the source of who you are. This source provides the power, courage and intention to achieve.

The purpose of this book is to encourage you to examine your foundation, the fountainhead of your thinking, the ground zero of your being, the birthplace of your every decision — the source of who you are.

In my experience, I have consistently found a set of principles and beliefs among individuals who are successful in both their work and their personal lives. Taking the time to examine and then reflect on these principles will offer new insight into your professional and personal decision making, allowing you to manage your business and life more productively.

I suggest you read each page and then consider it carefully. Ask yourself: *How does this concept apply to me? How am I operating according to this principle? What do I see that I have never seen before? What insights am I gaining? Have I sold out? Have I missed out? Am I on track? Is my business on track? What do I need to do in my enterprise to make this principle take hold?*

The Chinese characters are pictographs of these principles. They are intended to help you reflect on how the whole is made up of smaller elements and that multiple meanings may arise from the same source. This is about being open to new perspectives.

Acknowledging and understanding these principles will not only help you run a more successful business, but will help you become a more thoughtful human being — more grateful, more powerful and more fully alive. And where you begin this journey is at the very source of who you are and what you are working to become.

Dr. Marc B. Cooper

POSSIBILITY · 1
Possibility · Vision · Purpose · Intention
Mission · Transformation

INTEGRITY · 15
Integrity · Core Values · Responsibility
Commitment · Promises · Trust

CHARACTER · 29
Character · Courage · Taking a Stand
Service · Listening · Ownership
Leadership · Management · Coaching

CONTEXT · 49
Context · Information · Language
The Present · Distinctions · Competition
Problems · Breakdowns

ACCOUNTABILITY · 67
Accountability · Measurement · Results
Mindfulness · Power vs. Force

THANKFULNESS · 79
Thankfulness · Acknowledgement

Acknowledgements · 85

Dr. Marc Cooper Bio · 87

POSSIBILITY

Possibility is the SOURCE of the future.

Any future to be realized has possibility as its source. Possibility is the headwater of vision and achievement and the gateway to opportunity.

Stop thinking in terms of limitations and start thinking in terms of possibilities.

TERRY JOSEPHSON

POSSIBILITY

Possibility is a future that is conceivable, believable and achievable.

Possibility is required for any dream, any endeavor, any mission to be fulfilled.

Possibility is a person's first step towards commitment.

Possibility changes the way you see your circumstances and yourself.

Possibility is what leaders speak. It is the language of inspiration and innovation.

Possibility excites imagination and ignites potential.

Possibility offers new freedoms to be and new opportunities for action.

Possibility keeps you and your business from stagnation.

When stuck, create a possibility and reimagine yourself and the future.

Vision without action is a dream.
Action without vision is simply passing the time.
Action with vision is making a positive difference.

JOEL BARKER

VISION

Vision is a clearly articulated future.

Vision is a change that you completely believe will make a positive and lasting difference.

Vision moves people to see what can and needs to be accomplished.

Vision generates faith, hope and courage.

Vision inspires commitment and leads to effective action.

Vision replaces personal agendas with a mutually shared future. An authentic vision is never about you.

Have you seen the future? What is your vision?

*The greatest use of life is to spend it
for something that outlasts it.*

WILLIAM JAMES

PURPOSE

Purpose is the reason your enterprise exists. It is the essential motive for your business.

Purpose enables you to constantly and courageously battle the down-side risks.

Purpose is the guiding light that gives you direction — day after day, year after year.

Purpose gives you the power to keep on pushing and never give up.

Purpose is the ultimate adviser to setting your goals, targets and objectives.

Purpose gives meaning to your work.

Purpose gives meaning to your life.

> *Get yourself and your people on purpose — every day.*

Live with intention. Walk to the edge. Listen hard.
Practice wellness. Play with abandon. Laugh.
Choose with no regret. Appreciate your friends.
Continue to learn. Do what you love.
Live as if this is all there is.

MARY ANNE RADMACHER

INTENTION

Intention is your will — highly focused and clearly expressed.

Intention is the continuous application of your attention and energy to accomplish and achieve.

Intention is the driving force that centers you in taking appropriate action.

Intention eliminates distractions and reduces the influence of unfavorable circumstances.

Intention enables you to do what must be done.

Intention is single-mindedness.

Intention provokes you to do the right thing, even if you do not want to.

> *When breakdowns occur, always check your intention before you jump to intervention.*

When you discover your mission, you will feel its demand. It will fill you with enthusiasm and a burning desire to get to work on it.

W. CLEMENT STONE

MISSION

Mission makes the vision actionable.

Mission tightens purpose and unleashes passion.

Mission enables people to undertake heroic action to produce results.

Mission encourages you and your people to align, commit and act.

Mission allows people to make a difference and feel worthy.

Mission forces people out of the stands and onto the court.

Mission can always be expressed in goals and targets.

Mission has a definite beginning, middle and end.

> *Express your mission clearly and act with purpose.*

*Personal transformation can
and does have global effects.
As we go, so goes the world,
for the world is us.*

MARIANNE WILLIAMSON

TRANSFORMATION

Transformation is not simply change. It is something totally new.

Transformation is an internal revolution, breaking the bonds of who you have been.

Transformation is willingly operating beyond your past.

Transformation is becoming what your vision calls you to be in order to succeed.

Transformation requires you to displace what your own mind and others tell you cannot be.

Transformation occurs by taking a stand, making promises and then keeping your word.

Transformation is lasting only if it is conscious, intentional and purposeful.

Challenge the past and present to transform your future.

INTEGRITY

Integrity is the SOURCE of expression.

Integrity is expressed through trust.
This expression has no hypocrisy, pretense,
posturing, insincerity, deceit, or sanctimony in it.
The higher the level of integrity, the greater the loyalty
and effective performance of those around you.
The higher the level of integrity,
the greater the level of results.

*Have the courage to say 'No.'
Have the courage to face the truth.
Do the right thing because it is right.
These are the magic keys to living
your life with integrity.*

W. CLEMENT STONE

INTEGRITY

Integrity is all there is — all the time, every time.

Integrity is giving your word and keeping it. It is honoring yourself as your word.

Integrity is spoken as a promise. To elicit a promise from another is a request. Promises and requests are the language of integrity.

Integrity is your word in action. When you operate consistent with your word, the doer and the deed become one.

Integrity is the heart of success. Operate your business with and inside integrity. Interact with your employees from integrity. Interact with your customers with integrity. Interact with your vendors and suppliers with integrity. Hardest of all, interact with your competitors with integrity.

Have integrity. Hold yourself and your enterprise to your word — no matter what.

*If there are no common values,
there can be no image of the future.*

ROBERT BUNDY

CORE VALUES

Core values determine how you decide.

Core values determine how you act.

Core values determine your relationships.

Core values are primary; they are unchangeable, immutable and absolute. No matter what changes occur in the outside world, you will stand for these values.

Core values are the foundation you build your life and career around. They are always present and always operational.

Core values are embraced even when there is no reward. You abide by these values, no matter what the situation.

Take time, take stock, be honest.
Your core values define you.

Nobody ever did, or ever will, escape the consequences of his choices.

ALFRED A. MONTAPERT

RESPONSIBILITY

Responsibility is telling the truth to oneself.

Responsibility is holding yourself as cause in the matter. You see yourself as the source, the basis, the foundation for your actions and your outcomes.

Responsibility is a stand you take. It means looking at yourself first for why things are the way they are.

Responsibility is the antithesis of blame. Responsibility is never about faulting someone or something for why things turned out the way they did.

Responsibility begins with making a choice. Do I deliver on what I say or not? Do I lie or tell the truth? Do I make promises or excuses? Do I blame others or do I stand by my decisions and actions?

Be responsible for your successes.
Be responsible for your failures.

The quality of a person's life is in direct proportion to their commitment to excellence, regardless of their chosen field of endeavor.

VINCE LOMBARDI

COMMITMENT

Commitment is being your promise. It is being honor-bound to your word.

Commitment enables you to dedicate yourself to be faithful to your word in order to achieve your objective.

Commitment made only to yourself has little power.

Commitment made to another has more power. Commitment made to someone who is dedicated to your success has the most power of all.

Commitment enables you to face problems with more courage and authority. It empowers you to persevere in the face of failure or poor results.

Commitment shows up in two places: your calendar and your check book.

In all you endeavor, make a commitment to succeed.

Promises are the uniquely human way of ordering the future, making it predictable and reliable to the extent that this is humanly possible.

HANNAH ARENDT

PROMISES

Promises are your integrity spoken.

Promises are giving your word to a future and committing to make that future happen. They are spoken in the future tense and are your fullest intention expressed.

Promises reorient you to the circumstances facing you, so you have power. Promises allow you to adjust to and overcome the circumstances ahead of you.

Promises empower. Promises generate courage, tenacity and drive. They circumvent your ego and identity and allow you to operate as your highest self.

Promises require specificity. The clearer and more time-anchored your promise, the more powerful the promise.

Make legitimate promises and keep them.

I know God will not give me anything I can't handle. I just wish He didn't trust me so much.

MOTHER TERESA OF CALCUTTA

TRUST

Trust is a gift. Trust bestows confidence, belief, faith, assurance, certainty, conviction, reliance.

Trust begins with self. Unless you trust yourself first, you will not trust others. Learn to know yourself and then follow your heart.

Trust breeds loyalty. Superior teamwork and business longevity are hallmarks of trust.

Trust is at the center of creativity and innovation.

Trust can be displaced by control. The more control you apply, the more you risk losing trust. Distrust is stifling and cripples an enterprise.

Trust wisely. You may sometimes be deceived by trusting too much, but, if you trust too little, you will certainly cheat yourself of happiness.

Trust that people want to be trusted.

CHARACTER

Character is the SOURCE of self.

Character is the expression of your moral code and establishes your standards. It shapes your personal and professional rules of behavior. Character determines how you decide.

Fame is a vapor, popularity an accident, riches take wing, and only character endures.

HORACE GREELEY

CHARACTER

Character ultimately is who you are.

Character is built on core values, erected on fundamental beliefs and establishes how you act in the world.

Character discloses your true purpose. It determines what you choose or avoid.

Character, not the situation, issue or circumstance, makes the person. It is who you are when no one is looking.

Character does not require success, applause or admiration.

> *Character is not a result of fate, chance, luck or karma. Character is self determined.*

You gain strength, courage, and confidence by every experience in which you really stop to look fear in the face. You must do the thing which you think you cannot do.

ELEANOR ROOSEVELT

COURAGE

Courage is staring down uncertainty.

Courage is the greatest test of self. It plumbs one's very soul. If you act in your own self interest, it is not an act of courage.

Courage always moves beyond the purely rational to the fundamentally spiritual.

Courage is not the absence of fear or a resistance to fear. Courage is operating in spite of fear.

Courage produces calm and stores energy for decisive action.

Courage creates a sense of sanctuary. When we feel safe, we are much more able, more effective, and more self-expressed.

> *Be courageous and be at peace when challenges or conflicts arise.*

*If you stand up and be counted,
from time to time you may get
yourself knocked down.
But remember this:*
*A man flattened by an opponent can get up again.
A man flattened by conformity stays down for good.*

THOMAS J. WATSON

TAKING A STAND

Taking a stand is an existential act of courage. It is risky to bring something into existence, to bring something into the world that has not existed before.

Taking a stand means the balance of evidence is against you. There is no risk-free way of taking a stand.

Taking a stand always confronts current beliefs. It is you, standing for something that does not exist in the world.

Taking a stand takes high intention. It takes a willingness to put yourself at-stake for your stand.

Be willing to risk having your stand become real in the world.

*I don't know what your destiny
will be, but one thing I do know:
the only ones among you who
will be really happy are those
who have sought and found
how to serve.*

ALBERT SCHWEITZER

SERVICE

Service is leadership in its humblest and most effective form.

Service is an act of unselfishness, generosity, kindness and thoughtfulness.

Service is a commitment to dispel any discomfort, uneasiness, worry or distress.

Service is fully anticipating and totally meeting the needs of others.

Service is going above and beyond what the customer expects, time after time.

Service is providing focused attention to such a level that the customer is touched.

Service is being fully available, attentive, ready to act and singularly centered on the customer.

Take your attention off yourself and be in service to others.

To listen well, is as powerful a means of influence as to talk well, and is as essential to all true conversation.

CHINESE PROVERB

LISTENING

Listening is more powerful than speaking.

Listening is a selfless act of acknowledgement and appreciation.

Listening not only determines what is heard, but what is said.

Listening is stillness. It requires focus and concentration. It is the key to powerful communication.

Listening is necessary for successful and productive relationships.

Listening enables another to be who they want to be. It is the respectful recognition of another's worth.

Listening, not just speaking, opens the door to a shared future.

Stop, listen, acknowledge.

No man but feels more of a man in the world if he has a bit of ground that he can call his own. However small it is on the surface, it is four thousand miles deep; and that is a very handsome property.

CHARLES DUDLEY WARNER

OWNERSHIP

Ownership is all about legacy.

Ownership has the final say on the future.

Ownership is concerned with the long run. It is about making a lasting difference. While managers think in terms of hours, days and months, owners think in terms of years and decades — possibly centuries.

Ownership requires toughness, rigor and perseverance. Owners are relentless about making the future happen.

Ownership is about risk. Owners must be wholly invested in the enterprise. Owners never, never give up.

What legacy will you leave?

*Leadership can be thought of
as a capacity to define oneself
to others in a way that clarifies
and expands a vision of the future.*

EDWIN H. FRIEDMAN

LEADERSHIP

Leadership is a verb. It is action.

Leadership is spoken — a kind of speaking that brings forth a better future seen by all as possible. Leaders articulate this future in a way that produces enthusiasm, commitment and loyalty.

Leadership calls on people to be and do more than they thought possible of themselves. Leaders inspire others to aspire.

Leadership is never about ego. It is never about being right.

Leadership is being unconditionally committed to a vision and seeing it through.

Speak in the future tense and go lead.

*The conventional definition of management
is getting work done through people,
but real management is developing
people through work.*

AGHA HASAN ABEDI

MANAGEMENT

Management develops people through their work. It encourages them to be responsible. Pressuring, dictating and manipulating are the tactics of tyrants, not managers.

Management is a conversation which generates effective action in others so goals can be reached. It is a language of praise and empowerment, not complaint or judgment.

Management focuses on alignment, working to produce tangible outcomes by providing the right conditions.

Management gets paid for results. It deals with the complexity of business.

Go develop great employees and produce great results.

A good coach will make his players see what they can be rather than what they are.

ARA PARASHEGHIAN

COACHING

Coaching is a uniquely personal way of interacting with an individual that enables that person to perform at their highest level, beyond even what he or she believes is possible.

Coaching is being fully committed to the individual's best performance.

Coaching is defining the individual's performance by measurable outcomes and tangible accomplishments.

Coaching is removing those internal obstacles that prevent the individual from performing at his or her best.

Coaching possesses an intuition about the individual. For a coach to be effective, he or she must have a profound insight into what makes the individual tick.

Become a coach: Learn to recognize and eliminate the barriers to success for your team.

CONTEXT

Context is the SOURCE of perspective.

Context is decisive. Context determines
not only what is known, but also the way it is
known. Context regulates your perceptions, dictates
your understanding of the world and directs,
governs and molds what you see.

Priority is a function of context.

STEPHEN R. COVEY

CONTEXT

Context is decisive.

Context is the environment in which you and your business operate. It is the macro weather and the micro climate you experience every day.

Context rules. It determines what succeeds and what fails.

Context determines whether thoughts and actions will triumph or meet with disaster. Anything you try that is not supported by the context will not work.

Context forms the culture of the business. To shift the context, change the language within your business.

> *If something is not working, look at the context first and then re-examine your priorities.*

In your thirst for knowledge, be sure not to drown in all the information.

ANTHONY D'ANGELO

INFORMATION

Information by itself has no power.

Information must be combined with experience to become usable knowledge.

Information spoken, at best, turns into understanding. Yet, understanding does not necessarily incite action.

Information does not change behavior or thinking. You will not always produce results with information alone.

Information is foundational, but it cannot build by itself. Information needs commitment to become a constructive force in business.

Information has to be matched with a purpose, a goal, a personality. Then, it produces for the bottom line.

Without a clear purpose, information produces reasons not results. Stop explaining and start delivering results.

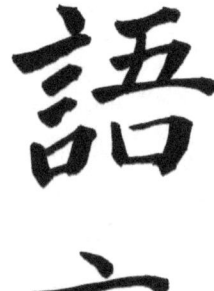

*Language exerts hidden power,
like a moon on the tides.*

RITA MAE BROWN

LANGUAGE

Language determines your being, your thinking and your culture. Human beings belong to language. We are born into language and become the language.

Language forms your context. Context determines your perceptions. Perception defines your actions. Actions decide the results.

Language is learned and can be re-learned. It is humankind's greatest tool.

Language is at the heart of most misunderstandings and subsequent problems or failures. Examine your words carefully and discover the language of success.

> *In business, language constitutes your business culture. Change the language, change the culture.*

Yesterday is history.
Tomorrow is a mystery.
And today?
Today is a gift.
That's why we
call it the present.

BABATUNDE OLATUNJI

珍惜現在

THE PRESENT

The present is all you have, really. The rest is memory, possibility or fantasy.

The present gives you power and a greater capacity to deal with what is so.

The present reduces the influence of the past, your psychology and your personality.

The present enhances your well being, your sense of wonder and your ability to respond appropriately. Enabling people to be in the present increases their focus, intention and attention.

The present quiets the mind, stops the chatter and reduces the noise. The more you and others can operate in the present, the greater the performance and, therefore, the greater the results.

Get yourself in the present — now.
Make sure you do the same for your staff.

In the sky, there is no distinction of east and west; people create distinctions out of their own minds and then believe them to be true.

BUDDHA

DISTINCTIONS

Distinctions are how you see the world.

Distinctions determine how you interpret your world.

Distinctions take things that are already there in the background and make them clear in the foreground.

Distinctions enable you to contrast things, to see variations, to differentiate and to divide one from another.

Distinctions observed in the key aspects of ownership, leadership, and management are critical to any enterprise's success.

Distinctions allow you to perceive people, trends, patterns and competition and markets in such a way that you can take effective action and be successful.

No distinction, no discernment,
no dividends.

*Live daringly, boldly, fearlessly.
Taste the relish to be found in
competition — in having put
forth the best within you.*

HENRY J. KAISER

COMPETITION

Competition is always moving the finish line.

Competition makes you better. It is always required for success.

Competition provides you with challenges that allow you to grow, overcome problems and work smarter.

Competition keeps your costs in line and makes you take better care of your employees.

Competition does not let you get arrogant, over-confident or lazy.

> *Send your competition a mental "Thank You" note. Without them, you might be ordinary.*

We can't solve problems by using the same kind of thinking we used when we created them.

ALBERT EINSTEIN

PROBLEMS

Problems are issues you blame yourself or others for.

Problems only go away if you take responsibility for them.

Problems should never be left unaddressed in order for you to be right. Do not keep problems around because you do not want to be responsible.

Problems confronted quickly and directly strengthen resolve and mitigate loss. If you condemn their very existence, you will never confront and conquer them.

Problems are why we have each other.

> *Do not be the problem when problems arise. Meet it, greet it and own it.*

Sometimes a breakdown can be the beginning of a kind of breakthrough, a way of living in advance through a trauma that prepares you for a future of radical transformation.

CHERRIE MORAGA

BREAKDOWNS

Breakdowns provide access to the future.

Breakdowns are temporary and time dependent. A problem is more invasive and personal.

Breakdowns tell you when your process or system is not working.

Breakdowns tell you when an employee is under performing or failing.

Breakdowns tell you when your plans or strategies need reassessment.

Breakdowns reveal your customer service mistakes.

Breakdowns can become your ally if you shift your relationship to them. They can be your canary in the coal mine and head off bigger problems.

Embrace your breakdowns and glimpse the future.

ACCOUNTABILITY

Accountability is the SOURCE of results.

Accountability is a place you stand. Accountability is who you are, not what you do. It is the source of effective action and, therefore, the essential ingredient for results.

*It is not only what we do,
but also what we do not do,
for which we are accountable.*

MOLIERE

ACCOUNTABILITY

Accountability is ground zero.

Accountability defines the lines on the court.

Accountability is neither time nor location dependent. You are always accountable.

Accountability requires a relationship. You cannot be accountable to yourself. You need to be accountable to another, someone who will hold you to account.

Accountability can be determined by asking four questions. *What are the core activities you are responsible for? What are the expected outcomes from these activities? How will your success in these activities be measured? What conditions do you need in place to be successful in these activities?*

Surround yourself with people who want to be accountable and get out of the way.

The only man who behaved sensibly was my tailor; he took my measurement anew every time he saw me, while all the rest went on with their old measurements and expected them to fit me.

GEORGE BERNARD SHAW

MEASUREMENT

Measurement forces you to focus, and whatever you focus on expands.

Measurement transforms the subjective into the objective. Measurement is to change, as light is to vision. Each enables you to see more clearly.

Measurement enables you to gauge the effectiveness of your actions and the accuracy of your strategy. In business and in life, you get what you measure.

Measuring is how you get to the bottom line. Numbers don't care how you feel. Numbers don't care about what you want. Numbers set you straight.

Measurement gives you something to test yourself against and to judge your success.

Before taking any corrective action, measure thoroughly.

*However beautiful the strategy,
you should occasionally
look at the results.*

WINSTON CHURCHILL

RESULTS

Results are a function of integrity and structure.

Results are tangible, measurable and should be mutually agreed upon.

Results are a product of effective action set into motion by committed individuals. Results are generated from promises kept.

Results are the achievement of the combined effort of each individual. Failure to deliver a result does not make you a failure.

Results are delivered through hard work. Results are not produced through hope, expectation or positive thinking. Optimism does not produce results — you do.

Get tangible. Get committed people.
Get results.

*The habit of ignoring our present moments
in favor of others yet to come leads directly
to a pervasive lack of awareness of the
web of life in which we are embedded.*

JON KABAT-ZINN

MINDFULNESS

Mindfulness is the capacity to be aware, conscious, alert and heedful of a situation or circumstance you are in.

Mindfulness is noticing. The range of what we think and do is limited by what we fail to notice. Being mindful allows you to remember fully.

Mindfulness is being awakened by possibility.

Mindfulness allows you to see the seams on the ball and slow the ball down so you can hit it.

Mindfulness allows you to be here now. It dims the past and the future.

Mindfulness of your industry, your enterprise, your people, your circumstances and your self all directly correlate to success.

> *Be mindful of what you are missing when you dwell on the past or fret about the future.*

Knowing others is wisdom;
Knowing the self is enlightenment;
Mastering others requires force;
Mastering the self needs strength.

LAO TZU

POWER VS. FORCE

Power is giving. **Force** is taking.

Power is about having others win. **Force** is about you winning.

Power is converting people's potential into performance. **Force** is pressuring people to perform.

Power is seeing what others need and want and giving them that. **Force** is seeing what you want and extracting that from others.

Power is doing the right thing, at the right time for others. **Force** is doing whatever it takes without regard for others.

Power is promoting, acknowledging, supporting and allowing people to choose. **Force** is oppressing, harassing, intimidating, and pressuring others for your own needs.

If you are using force, you have no real power.

THANKFULNESS

Thankfulness is the SOURCE of satisfaction.

Being thankful ignites gratitude and
fans the flame of selflessness and humility.
It promotes you being more accessible
and stokes the embers of satisfaction.

*If Thank You is the
only prayer you say,
that will be enough.*

MEISTER ECKHART

THANKFULNESS

Thankfulness is being filled with gratitude. Be thankful for what you have; you'll end up having more. If you focus on what you don't have, you will never have enough.

Thankfulness is being appreciative of who you are and what you have. What you appreciate appreciates.

Thankfulness is a choice and you have three choices in life: tolerate, change or be grateful.

Thank You acknowledges another's contribution. More importantly, Thank You acknowledges the person who made the contribution.

Freedom consists not in refusing to recognize anything above us, but in respecting something which is above us; for by respecting it, we raise ourselves to it, and, by our very acknowledgment, prove that we bear within ourselves what is higher, and are worthy to be on a level with it.

JOHANN WOLFGANG
VON GOETHE

ACKNOWLEDGEMENT

Acknowledgement allows a person to be known, honored, appreciated and loved.

Acknowledgement is always longed for, but rarely asked for.

Acknowledgement lets someone know they make a difference — for you, for your enterprise and the people it serves.

Acknowledgement is the highest level of request.

Speak up and acknowledge. Recognize the contributions of others.

Acknowledgements

Who you are, and who you become is a direct result of your relationships. To my teachers, clients, coaches and colleagues, people who constitute my world and make it possible.

To my wife and life-partner Leslie Copland, who empowers me to be my highest self.

To Chris Creamer whose talent made the publishing of this book possible.

To Jue Pu, whose calligraphy brings a dimension of beauty and contemplation.

To Angela Ekstowicz who manages me, so results and outcomes are produced.

To Matt King, whose remarkable editing tunes the message, allowing its full power to be expressed.

Thank you for your contributions to this book, to our work, and for enabling me to make a difference.

DR. MARC COOPER

Dr. Marc B. Cooper's background of experience includes post-doctoral student, academician, basic science researcher, associate professor, private practitioner, business owner, independent contractor, author, poet, organizational developer, trainer, seminar director, executive coach, life coach, blogger, speaker, inventor, board director, elder, mentor, futurist, dog owner, husband, father, grandfather, and human being.

www.seeking-wisdom.com

www.ingramcontent.com/pod-product-compliance
Lightning Source LLC
Chambersburg PA
CBHW031448210526
45464CB00005B/2372